Learn a Language!

See and Say Vietnamese

by Tran Thi Minh Phuoc

PEBBLE
a capstone imprint

Published by Pebble, an imprint of Capstone
1710 Roe Crest Drive, North Mankato, Minnesota 56003
capstonepub.com

Library of Congress Cataloging-in-Publication Data is available on the Library of Congress website.
ISBN: 9780756587574 (hardcover)
ISBN: 9780756587529 (paperback)
ISBN: 9780756587536 (ebook PDF)

Summary: How do you tell someone about your hobbies in Vietnamese? What's the Vietnamese word for *library*? With this book, curious kids will see and say simple words and phrases in Vietnamese.

Editorial Credits
Editor: Ericka Smith; Designer: Sarah Bennett; Media Researcher: Svetlana Zhurkin; Production Specialist: Katy LaVigne

Image Credits
Dreamstime: Hoxuanhuong, 11 (top right), Ke Nguyen, 11 (top left); Getty Images: chomnancoffee, 17 (top right), DragonImages, 22 (bottom right), hadynyah, 20 (top), JethuynhCan, 13 (top left), kate_sept2004, 22 (top left), leonovo, 27 (top), lirtlon, 12 (top right), Nick Dolding, 26 (middle), SunnyVMD, 9 (top), 14 (bottom), Tatiana Terekhina, 11 (middle right), Tdo, 25 (bottom left); Shutterstock: A3pfamily, 6, aappp, 21 (top), aDam Wildlife, 12 (bottom left), Alberto Urbano Martinez, 26 (top), Alexlukin, 17 (middle), Anurak Pongpatimet, 26 (bottom), AS Foodstudio, 10 (bottom), asife, 31 (middle), beibaoke, 20 (bottom), bergamont, 29 (middle right), Bob Pool, 18 (top left), Boonchuay Promjiam, 29 (bottom left), Bowmf, 18 (bottom left), Danny Ye, 19 (top left), DnD-Production, 13 (bottom left), Dragon Images, 8, 9 (bottom), 19 (top right), Ekkasit A Siam, 23 (top right), Elizabeth_0102, 29 (middle left), Eric Isselee, 13 (top right, middle right), FamVeld, 30 (middle left), Fascinadora, 30 (middle), Fotofermer, 28 (bottom left), godongphoto, 19 (middle), halimqd (speech bubble and burst), cover and throughout, Hong Vo, 16 (bottom), huntergol hp, 19 (bottom left), Huy Thoai, 4 (bottom), 25 (top right), I love photo, 22 (top right), inewsfoto, 11 (bottom left), Irina Wilhauk, 31 (top), karins, 11 (bottom right), Kurit afshen, 13 (bottom right), Kwadrat, 12 (bottom right), Luong Led, 18 (top right), Magnia (lined texture), cover and throughout, Makistock, 7 (bottom left), Minh Quan Du, 4 (top), Nataly Studio, cover (top left), Natalya Aksenova, 13 (middle left), Naypong Studio, cover (top right), 29 (top), Nikkikii, 7 (bottom right), Nina Lishchuk, 7 (top), nukeaf, 24, oksana2010, 28 (top right), OlegD, 11 (milk), oodles, 12 (top left), Pixel-Shot, 16 (top left and right), Prostock-studio, 7 (middle), Q88, 4 (middle), 17 (top left), 23 (bottom), Qcon, 21 (middle), Quang Ho, 10 (top), Ronnachai Palas, cover (bottom right), 1, Russell Savage, 27 (bottom), Ruth Black, 30 (top, middle right, bottom), 31 (middle right, middle left, bottom), Ryan Photo Capture, 20 (middle), spiharu.u (spot line art), cover and throughout, ssuaphotos, cover (bottom left), StreetVJ, 18 (bottom right), swissmacky, 17 (bottom), Tanes Ngamsom, 21 (bottom), thi, 25 (top left), Tim UR, 28 (top left), TinnaPong, 15 (middle), 23 (top left), Trieu Nhat Le, 19 (bottom right), Tuan Anh Vu, 14 (top), 15 (top, bottom), Vangert, 28 (bottom right), Vietnam Stock Images, 25 (bottom right), vungnn, 11 (middle left), Waridsara_HappyChildren, 22 (bottom left), winphong, 29 (bottom right), yevgeniy11, cover (middle left)

Pronunciations for this book were created using a pronunciation guide created by Tri C. Tran, PhD.

Printed and bound in China. 6096

Table of Contents

The Vietnamese Language

Tiếng Việt (tyehng vyeht), or Vietnamese, is the official language of Việt Nam (Vietnam). There are three main dialects—or forms—of the language: northern Vietnamese, central Vietnamese, and southern Vietnamese. In this book, you'll learn the southern Vietnamese dialect.

How to Use This Book

Some words and phrases complete a sentence. Those will appear in bold.

English **I like . . .**
Vietnamese Tôi thích . . .
Say It! tohy theech

+

English **dancing.**
Vietnamese khiêu vũ.
Say It! khyeh voo

Others give you the name for a person, place, thing, or idea.

English spring
Vietnamese mùa xuân
Say It! moo-uh soo-uhn

Meet Chatty Cat! Chatty Cat will show you how to say the words and phrases in this book.

Vietnamese Vowels and Tones

Vietnamese has 12 vowels. Some have accent marks to show the sound it makes.

Vowel Sounds										
a	ă	â	e	ê	i, y	o	ô	ơ	u	ư
like in f**a**ther	like in c**a**t	like *u* in **u**nder	like in t**e**nt	like *a* in **a**te	like *e* in m**e**	like *aw* in l**aw**	like in n**o**	like *u* in f**u**r	like *oo* in m**oo**	like in b**u**tter

Vietnamese has six tones. Five use accent marks that look like how the sound changes. When you see a vowel with one of the marks below, use this guide to help you say the word.

Mark	How to Pronounce	Example	Pronunciation
None	one high tone	la	→ lahhh
´	start high, get higher	lá	↗ la-aah
~	start high, get higher, but broken up	lã	↗ ↗ lah-ah
ˀ	start low, get higher	lả	↗ laa-ah
`	start low, get lower	là	↘ la-aah
.	low and quick	lạ	→ lah

Some words, like *rất*, have vowels with more than one accent mark that show you how to pronounce the word.

rất = r + uh + t

For *rất*, you'd say "rut" with a high tone that gets higher.

Greetings and Common Phrases

Vietnamese Những Lời Chào Hỏi và Các Câu Thông Dụng

Say It! nhung luhy chahw hoy vah kahk kohw thohngm yoongm

English Hello!
Vietnamese (Xin) chào!
Say It! (seen) chahw

English My name is . . .
Vietnamese Tôi tên là . . .
Say It! tohy tehn lah

English What is your name?
Vietnamese Bạn tên gì?
Say It! bahn tehn yee

English How are you?
Vietnamese Bạn khỏe không?
Say It! bahn kweh khohngm

English I am fine.
Vietnamese Tôi khỏe.
Say It! tohy kweh

English Nice to meet you.
Vietnamese Rất vui được gặp bạn.
Say It! rut voo-ee duhk gahp bahn

English Please.
Vietnamese Xin vui lòng.
Say It! seen voo-ee lahng

English Thank you!
Vietnamese Cảm ơn!
Say It! kam uhn

English You’re welcome!
Vietnamese Không có chi!
Say It! khohngm kah chee

English Goodbye!
Vietnamese (Xin) chào!
Say It! (seen) chahw

English See you later!
Vietnamese Hẹn gặp lại!
Say It! hen gahp lie

English Yes.
Vietnamese Có.
Say It! kah

English No.
Vietnamese Không.
Say It! khohngm

In Vietnam, “Xin chào” is a polite, respectful greeting used in formal situations, like when someone greets a parent or a teacher. When someone talks to a person they know well, they just say “Chào.” But neither greeting can be used with just someone’s name. Instead, they might use these greeting to say “Hello, friend” or “Goodbye, teacher.”

Family

Vietnamese Gia Đình

Say It! 😺 yah deenh

English **This is . . .**

Vietnamese Đây là . . .

Say It! 😺 day lah

English **my father.**

Vietnamese ba tôi.

Say It! 😺 bah tohy

English **my mother.**

Vietnamese má tôi.

Say It! 😺 mah tohy

English **my sibling.**

Vietnamese anh chị em tôi.

Say It! 😺 anh chee em tohy

English **my sister.**

Vietnamese chị tôi. (older)

Say It! 😺 chee tohy

Vietnamese em gái tôi. (younger)

Say It! 😺 em gahy tohy

English **my brother.**

Vietnamese anh tôi. (older)

Say It! 😺 anh tohy

Vietnamese em trai tôi. (younger)

Say It! 😺 em trie tohy

English **my aunt.**

Vietnamese cô tôi. (father's side)

Say It! 🐱 koh tohy

Vietnamese dì tôi. (mother's side)

Say It! 🐱 yee tohy

English **my uncle.**

Vietnamese chú tôi. (father's side)

Say It! 🐱 choo tohy

Vietnamese cậu tôi. (mother's side)

Say It! 🐱 kohw tohy

English **my cousin.**

Vietnamese anh chị em họ tôi.

Say It! 🐱 anh chee em hah tohy

English **my grandmother.**

Vietnamese bà nội tôi. (father's side)

Say It! 🐱 bah nohy tohy

Vietnamese bà ngoại tôi. (mother's side)

Say It! 🐱 bah ngwahy tohy

English **my grandfather.**

Vietnamese ông nội tôi. (father's side)

Say It! 🐱 ohngm nohy tohy

Vietnamese ông ngoại tôi. (mother's side)

Say It! 🐱 ohngm ngwahy tohy

Food

Vietnamese Thức Ăn

Say It! 🐱 tuk ahn

English **I'm hungry. I want . . .**

Vietnamese Tôi đói. Tôi muốn . . .

Say It! 🐱 tohy doy tohy mwohn

English **breakfast.**

Vietnamese ăn sáng.

Say It! 🐱 ahn sahng

English mung bean sticky rice

Vietnamese xôi đậu xanh

Say It! 🐱 sohy dohw sanh

English **lunch.**

Vietnamese ăn trưa.

Say It! 🐱 ahn truuh

English broken rice with grilled meat

Vietnamese cơm tấm với thịt nướng

Say It! 🐱 kuhm tahm vuhy tit nuuhng

English **dinner.**
Vietnamese ăn tối.
Say It! 🐱 ahn tohy

English fried fish with boiled vegetables
Vietnamese cá chiên với rau luộc
Say It! 🐱 kah chyehn vuhy rao lwohk

English **a snack.**
Vietnamese món ăn vặt.
Say It! 🐱 mon ahn vaht

English coconut candy
Vietnamese kẹo dừa
Say It! 🐱 kew yuuh

English milk
Vietnamese sữa
Say It! 🐱 shuuh

English bread
Vietnamese bánh mì
Say It! 🐱 banh mee

English dragon fruit
Vietnamese trái thanh long
Say It! 🐱 trie thanh lahngm

English Malabar spinach
Vietnamese rau mồng tơi
Say It! 🐱 row mohngm tuhy

Animals

Vietnamese Động Vật

Say It! dohngm vaht

English a dog

Vietnamese con chó

Say It! kahn chah

English a water buffalo

Vietnamese con trâu

Say It! kahn trohw

English a bird

Vietnamese con chim

Say It! kahn cheem

English a horse

Vietnamese con ngựa

Say It! kahn nguuh

English a fish
Vietnamese con cá
Say It! kahn kah

English a pig
Vietnamese con heo
Say It! kahn hew

English a chicken
Vietnamese con gà
Say It! kahn gah

English a cat
Vietnamese con mèo
Say It! kahn mew

English a cow
Vietnamese con bò
Say It! kahn bah

English a frog
Vietnamese con ếch
Say It! kahn ehch

At Home

Vietnamese Ở Nhà

Say It! 😺 uh nyah

English kitchen

Vietnamese bếp

Say It! 😺 behp

English table

Vietnamese bàn

Say It! 😺 bahn

English chair

Vietnamese ghế

Say It! 😺 geh

English door

Vietnamese cửa

Say It! 😺 kuuh

English living room

Vietnamese phòng khách

Say It! 😺 fahngm khach

English computer

Vietnamese máy vi tính

Say It! 😺 mahy vee teenh

English couch

Vietnamese đi văng

Say It! 😺 dee vahng

English bedroom
Vietnamese phòng ngủ
Say It! fahngm ngoo

English bed
Vietnamese giường
Say It! yuuhng

English window
Vietnamese cửa sổ
Say It! kuuh soh

English cell phone
Vietnamese điên thoại di động
Say It! dyehn thwahy yee dohngm

English bathroom
Vietnamese phòng tắm
Say It! fahngm tahm

English sink
Vietnamese bồn rửa
Say It! bohn ruh-uh

English bathtub
Vietnamese bồn tắm
Say It! bohn tahm

English toilet
Vietnamese bồn cầu
Say It! bohn kohw

Clothing

Vietnamese Quần Áo

Say It! 😺 kwuhn ahw

English **I am wearing . . .**

Vietnamese Tôi mặc . . .

Say It! 😺 tohy măk

English **a shirt.**

Vietnamese áo sơ mi.

Say It! 😺 ahw shuh mee

English **a skirt.**

Vietnamese váy ngắn.

Say It! 😺 văy ngahn

English **a coat.**

Vietnamese áo khoác.

Say It! 😺 ahw kwahk

English **a Vietnamese long dress.**

Vietnamese áo dài.

Say It! 😺 ahw yie

English I am wearing shoes.

Vietnamese Tôi mang giầy.

Say It! 😺 tohy mang yah-ee

English **a sweatshirt.**

Vietnamese áo nỉ.

Say It! ahw nee

English **pants.**

Vietnamese quần.

Say It! kwuhn

English I am wearing a palm leaf conical hat.

Vietnamese Tôi đội nón lá.

Say It! tohy dohy nahn lah

English **a dress.**

Vietnamese áo đầm.

Say It! ahw duhm

English I am wearing socks.

Vietnamese Tôi mang vớ.

Say It! tohy mahng vuh

In Vietnamese, how you say "I am wearing" changes based on the item of clothing you are talking about.

In the Neighborhood

Vietnamese Trong Khu Phố

Say It! trahngm khoo foh

English school

Vietnamese trường học

Say It! truuhng halkp

English apartment building

Vietnamese chung cư

Say It! choongm kuh

English street

Vietnamese đường phố

Say It! duuhng foh

English house

Vietnamese căn nhà

Say It! kan nyah

English bus stop

Vietnamese trạm xe buýt

Say It! tram seh bweet

English post office

Vietnamese bưu điện

Say It! buuw dyehn

English library

Vietnamese thư viện

Say It! thuuh vyehn

English hospital

Vietnamese bệnh viện

Say It! behnh vyehn

English grocery store

Vietnamese tiệm tạp hóa

Say It! tyehm tap hwah

English a park

Vietnamese công viên

Say It! kohngm vyehn

Transportation

Vietnamese Vận Chuyển

Say It! vuhn choo-wehn

English boat

Vietnamese con thuyền

Say It! kahn thoo-wehn

English bus

Vietnamese chiếc xe buýt

Say It! chyehk seh bweet

English train

Vietnamese chiếc xe lửa

Say It! chyehk seh luuh

English airplane
Vietnamese chiếc máy bay
Say It! chyehk mahy bahy

English car
Vietnamese chiếc xe hơi
Say It! chyehk seh huhy

English a bicycle
Vietnamese chiếc xe đạp
Say It! chyehk seh dahp

English truck
Vietnamese chiếc xe tải
Say It! chyehk seh tie

Hobbies

Vietnamese Sở Thích

Say It! 🐱 shuh theech

English **I like . . .**

Vietnamese Tôi thích . . .

Say It! 🐱 tohy theech

English **cooking.**

Vietnamese nấu nướng.

Say It! 🐱 nohw nuuhng

English **swimming.**

Vietnamese bơi lội.

Say It! 🐱 buhy lohy

English **painting.**

Vietnamese vẽ.

Say It! 🐱 veh

English **singing.**

Vietnamese ca hát.

Say It! 🐱 kah haht

English **soccer.**

Vietnamese đá banh.

Say It! 🐱 dah banh

English ball

Vietnamese trái banh

Say It! 🐱 trie banh

English **reading.**

Vietnamese đọc.

Say It! 🐱 dahkp

English book

Vietnamese sách

Say It! 🐱 sahk

English **dancing.**

Vietnamese khiêu vũ.

Say It! 🐱 khyeh voo

Days of the Week

Vietnamese Các Ngày Trong Tuần

Say It! kahk ngahy trahngm twuhn

English **Today is . . .**

Vietnamese Hôm nay là ngày . . .

Say It! hohm nahy lah ngahy

English **Monday.**

Vietnamese Thứ hai.

Say It! thuuh hie

English **Tuesday.**

Vietnamese Thứ ba.

Say It! thuuh bah

English **Wednesday.**

Vietnamese Thứ tư.

Say It! thuuh tuuh

English **Thursday.**

Vietnamese Thứ năm.

Say It! thuuh nahm

English **Friday.**

Vietnamese Thứ sáu.

Say It! thuuh shaow

English **Saturday.**

Vietnamese Thứ bảy.

Say It! thuuh bahy

English **Sunday.**

Vietnamese Chủ nhật.

Say It! choo nhut

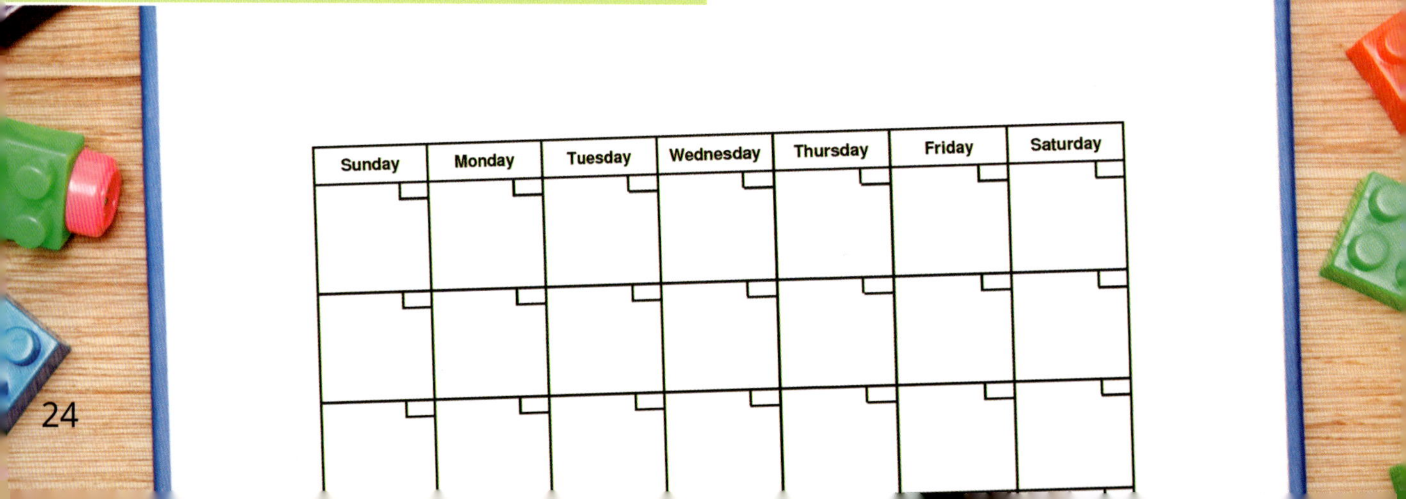

Seasons

Vietnamese Các Mùa

Say It! kak moo-uh

English winter

Vietnamese mùa đông

Say It! moo-uh doyngm

English spring

Vietnamese mùa xuân

Say It! moo-uh soo-uhn

English summer

Vietnamese mùa hè

Say It! moo-uh heh

English fall

Vietnamese mùa thu

Say It! moo-uh thoo

Weather

Vietnamese Thời Tiết

Say It! 🐱 thuhy tyeht

English **It is . . .**

Vietnamese Trời . . .

Say It! 🐱 truhy

English **windy.**

Vietnamese gió.

Say It! 🐱 yah

English **raining.**

Vietnamese mưa.

Say It! 🐱 muuh

English **cold.**

Vietnamese lạnh.

Say It! 🐱 lanh

English **snowing.**

Vietnamese tuyết.

Say It! 🐱 too-yet

English **hot.**
Vietnamese nóng.
Say It! 😺 nahngm

English **sunny.**
Vietnamese nắng.
Say It! 😺 nahng

English **cloudy.**
Vietnamese mây.
Say It! 😺 mahy

Colors

Vietnamese Màu Sắc

Say It! 🐱 maow sahk

English red

Vietnamese màu đỏ

Say It! 🐱 maow dah

English pink

Vietnamese màu hồng

Say It! 🐱 maow hohngm

English green

Vietnamese màu xanh lá cây

Say It! 🐱 maow sanh lah kahy

English orange

Vietnamese màu cam

Say It! 🐱 maow kahm

English blue
Vietnamese màu xanh da trời
Say It! 🐱 maow sanh yah truhy

English yellow
Vietnamese màu vàng
Say It! 🐱 maow vangm

English purple
Vietnamese màu tím
Say It! 🐱 maow teem

English black
Vietnamese màu đen
Say It! 🐱 maow dehn

English white
Vietnamese màu trắng
Say It! 🐱 maow tahng

Numbers

Vietnamese Con Số

Say It! 🐱 kahn shoh

1

English one

Vietnamese một

Say It! 🐱 moht

2

English two

Vietnamese hai

Say It! 🐱 hie

3

English three

Vietnamese ba

Say It! 🐱 bah

4

English four

Vietnamese bốn

Say It! 🐱 bohn

5

English five

Vietnamese năm

Say It! 🐱 nahm

6

English six

Vietnamese sáu

Say It! shaow

7

English seven

Vietnamese bảy

Say It! bahy

8

English eight

Vietnamese tám

Say It! tahm

9

English nine

Vietnamese chín

Say It! cheen

10

English ten

Vietnamese mười

Say It! muuhy

About the Translator

Trần Thị Minh Phước is a retired librarian, an award-winning author, and a respected storyteller. She shares her experiences and knowledge of Vietnamese culture at cultural events, storytelling programs, conferences, libraries, colleges, and schools throughout the United States. She lives in Minneapolis, Minnesota. For more information about Trần, please visit https://phuocthiminhtran.wordpress.com/.